Isabella's
Preserves

Front Cover Picture: Strawberry, Apricot and Tangerine Pavlova. See page 55.

Published by Maureen E..Forbes-Gray
Forbe-3
Milltimber, Aberdeen,Scotland

on behalf of Isabella's Preserves

ISBN   0 - 9533551 - 2 - 8

Cover Design   Stuart Johnstone, Photography and Visual Communication,
                      Gray's School of Art, The Robert Gordon's University, Aberdeen.
Cover Photography   Berry Bingel and Stuart Johnstone.
Designed by   Maureen Forbes-Gray, Alastair Massie, Isabella Massie.
Editor   Maureen Forbes-Gray.
Typeset   Léla Burgoyne   Maureen Forbes-Gray.
Proof Read By   Christopher J. Gray   Maureen Forbes-Gray.
Recipe Testing and Creation   Isabella Massie   Maureen Forbes-Gray.
Photograph of Hector by Alastair Massie

Printed and bound in Scotland by Polester AUP Aberdeen, Ltd.

Isabella's Cook Book

ALASTAIR AND ISABELLA MASSIE

OF

ISABELLA'S PRESERVES

Hector - the family pooch

PUBLISHER MAUREEN FORBES-GRAY
FORBE-3

This book is dedicated to
our daughters
Isabella and Carol-Ann
and our Grandaughter Flora

ACKNOWLEDGMENTS

Isabella's Cookbook was really conceived by loyal our customer's. Without their interest in the products and continual request for recipe ideas, the book may never have come to fruition. At the many shows and fairs we attend, we are constantly asked for recipes, the favourite being pancakes of which we make hundreds, to allow customers to taste our products. Not having any experience writing books, we sought the help of Maureen Forbes-Gray. Our families have been connected through the catering and farming world for over 20 years.

This book is the fifth cookery book which Maureen has published. She started publishing cookbooks to raise money for children in need. In particular, fund raising for the Autistic society. Having a child suffering from this condition, this has been a great inspiration to continue in this field.

From the time we had our first meeting in January 2003, Maureen has worked like a Trojan to achieve our deadline, of a June publication. Her experience in publishing and the cooking field has proved an invaluable resource to us. She has moved house during this time, and could not have achieved what she has, without the support of her husband Chris and children, Anna and Alexander. Betty Forbes her mother and Auntie Maggie have been a great support, as always in caring for the children for which we are very grateful.

The staff at the printers, Polestar AUP, have done a marvellous job,under difficult circumstances in getting the book printed. We would like to particularly thank David Barber and Léla Burgoyne, for the incredible support given to the project.

Many thanks to Berry Bingel and Stuart Johnstone the photographers, we did have fun with them, doing the food photography.

We have our long standing friend, Edi Swan to thank for the art illustrations.

Our small business has flourished over the last 5 years and this is due in no small way to the dedication of our staff. The girls in "the factory" are dedicated to ensure that the high quality of the products, are maintained at all times. One of our key workers, who is now 75 years old, has worked on the farm with us for over 20 years. She does all the labelling, cutting of the tartan ribbon, fitting it to the jars, and completing the final checks, before packing.

Finally we would like to thank our stockists and customers, who have enthusiastically supported us over the years.

All recipes in this cookbook generously feed 4-6 people.

Contents   Page

The Eight Page Colour Section

Weights and Measures

Always use either Metric or Imperial - It is best not to mix the two

Weight:
15g ($^1/_2$oz)
25g (1oz)
40g (1$^1/_2$oz)
50g (1$^3/_4$oz aprox.)
75g (3oz approx)
100g (3$^1/_2$oz exact)
125g (4oz)
150g (5$^1/_2$oz)
175g (6oz)
200g (7oz)
225g (8oz)
250g (9oz)
275g (9$^1/_2$ oz)
300g (10$^1/_2$oz)
325g (11$^1/_2$ oz)
350g (12oz)
375g (13oz)
400g (14oz)
425g (15oz)
450g (16oz)
500g (1lb 2oz)
600g (1lb 5oz)
750g (1lb 10oz)
1kg (2lbs or 2lb4oz exact)
2.25kg (5lb)

Volume:
15ml ($^1/_2$ fl.oz.)
25ml (1fl.oz.)
50ml (2fl.oz.)
75ml (3fl.oz. approx)
100ml (3fl.oz approx)
125ml (4 fl.oz.)
150ml (5fl.oz., $^1/_4$pt)
175ml (6fl.oz)
200 ml (7fl.oz. $^1/_3$pint)
250mls (9fl.oz)
300mls (10fl.oz.)
325ml (11 fl.oz.)
350ml (12fl.oz.)
400ml (14fl.oz.)
425ml (15fl.oz. $^3/_4$pint)
450ml (16fl.oz.)
475ml (17fl.oz.)
500ml (20fl.oz. approx)
600mls (20fl.oz. 1pt)
1L. (2pt approx)
1.2L. (2pts)
2L. (3$^1/_2$pts)
3L. (5$^1/_4$pts)

Introduction

Isabella and I met through the Young Farmer's Club, which must be one of the best matrimonial agencies in the country.

Isabella trained in Home Economics at the "Do School" in Aberdeen. After we married she joined me at our present home, Lower Braikley Farm. In the 1970's we started growing vegetables for the rapidly expanding market in Aberdeen Our first shop opened in Ellon, this was shortly followed by the 'Farmhouse' in Aberdeen. The shop employed 22 staff. We started to move into more exotic fruit's, stocking vegetables such as Avocado, Aubergines, Kiwi Fruit, and special Olive Oils. However by the mid-80's the larger supermarkets had a major presence in Aberdeen, competition was fierce, and the shop was purchased by Norco.

As a way of diversification, Isabella started cookery courses, and became Home Economist for Sainsbury's in Aberdeen. I developed a food consultancy, this included research work for the popular Grampian TV series "Scotland's Larder".

It was during this time in the early 90s, that Isabella's Wholegrain Mustard was discovered by a friend who suggested she put the product on the market. Armed with a few white buckets and a stainless steel spoon we started the business. In 1995, we went to the Royal Highland Show in Edinburgh and as luck would have it, one of our first visitors was a buyer from John Lewis. She ordered 180 dozen jars, and we were off and running. In the same year we went to the BBC Good Food Show in Birmingham and this time caught the eye of the condiments buyer for Waitrose, who ordered 840 dozen jars. This was quite a challenge with a few buckets and a spoon.

Soon thereafter, we started making a very successful Tomato Relish. Up until then we had been working in the farmhouse kitchen. We converted some farm buildings to create a professional kitchen with proper storage, which is fondly known as "The Factory". We now have 3 full time staff, and part-time help. The business has gone from strength to strength winning many awards. Isabella is continually developing new products which are innovative and distinctive.

We do hope you enjoy these recipes, many created by Isabella and Maureen, and some family favourites. Most of the recipes use Isabella's products, or can be complimented by them.

The Products

We are glad that we employ local people. Our eldest employee is 75 years old. She applies all our labels, and distinctive tartan ribbon by hand. Our ingredients are sourced locally where possible, we do not use any preservatives or additives.

Starting with the Wholegrain Mustard and Tomato Relish, we now have a range of over 33 products. At the Aviemore Trade Fair in1998, Chivas Brothers of Rothes, owners of Glen Grant Distillery, asked us to make apple jelly for them, using apples from their own orchard.
At the Highland Show in 1999 we won a Silver Medal with our Cinnamon and Apple Jelly. The publicity, led to an order for a range of jams and marmalades from Champany's Inn Linlithgow. The launch of this range led to 3 Great Taste Awards, with the Raspberry Jam winning the Gold Award, "The Best in Britain" Silver Awards were awarded for our Strawberry Jam and Seville Orange and Ginger Marmalade.
In 2000, we were asked by Donald Russell of Inverurie to produce a range of sauces to accompany their meats. Again this has proved to be a very popular range, especially the Hot Banana Chutney. In 2001 this product won a Silver medal at the Royal Highland Show and a Gold at the Grampian Food Awards.
The products are widely available throughout Scotland. A list of some of our stockists is available at the back of this cookery book. Stockists include Jenners of Edinburgh, House of Bruar, and Brodie Country Fayre. Some own label products are produced for other outlets such as Scottish Parliament and Balmoral. Our catering range of products is currently used by Gleneagles Hotel and The Marcliffe at Pitfodels in Aberdeen and other catering establishments

Alastair Massie
June 2003

IN THE BEGINNING

Tomato and Red Pepper Soup

with Basil Scones

910g (2lbs) Tomatoes
1 red pepper
1 medium onion finely chopped

25g (1oz) sugar
3fl.oz. dry sherry
50g (2oz) unsalted butter

Method
1. De-seed and core the pepper, under a hot grill, blister the skin. Place the pepper in a "poly" bag to cool. When cool peel the skin off and roughly chop.
2. In a frying pan, sauté the onion until opaque in colour.
3. Add all the other ingredients. Simmer for 45 minutes stirring occasionally.
4. Cool, liquidize and season to taste.
5. Re-heat for serving.

Basil Scones

500g (¹/₂lb) plain flour
1 tsp Cream of Tartar
¹/₂ tsp Bicarbonate of Soda
Pinch of salt

60g (2¹/₂oz) margarine
1 egg yolk
Milk to mix

Method
1. Heat the oven to a temperature of 400°F, 200°C, Gas 8.
2. Mix the dry ingredients, rub in the margarine until the mixture resembles fine bread crumbs, toss in a handful of torn basil leaves.
3. Blend the egg yolk and milk. Mix the dry and wet ingredients to form a soft dough. Roll out to 1″ thickness, cut with a 2″ round fluted cutter.
4. Bake at 200°F for 6-8 minutes. Serve warm with soup.

Cook's Note: *These freeze well, the basil retains it's beautiful green colour.*

Tomato, Pear and Horseradish Soup
Lady Claire Macdonald
Kinloch Lodge

3 tablsp olive oil
2 onions, skinned and chopped
1 stick celery, skin removed and sliced
1x14oz (400g) tin chopped tomatoes
2 ripe pears, with skin and core, but stalks
removed, chopped

2 pints (1.2 litres) good stock
1 tablsp Isabella's Horseradish Sauce
sea salt

Method

Heat the oil in a saucepan and saute the onions for a few minutes. Add the sliced celery and continue to cook until the onions are soft, and start to caramelize. Then add the chopped pears, the tomatoes, the stock and the horseradish sauce. Bring to simmering point,and cook gently for 5-10 minutes. Take off the heat, cool, then liquidize and sieve. Taste, and season with salt and pepper. To serve, reheat and garnish simply with a basil leaf or some chives on top of each helping.

Claire's Note: *The sweetness of the pear is counteracted by the sharpness of the horseradish. The soup may be made a couple of days in advance,providing it is kept in the fridge.*

Cucumber Mousse with Prawns

1 cucumber skinned and finely diced
400g Philadelphia cheese
1 package gelatine
1 tablsp chopped parsley

300ml ($\frac{1}{2}$ pint) lightly whipped cream
300ml ($\frac{1}{2}$ pint) chicken stock
1.25ml ($\frac{1}{4}$ tsp) onion juice
salt and pepper

Method

1. Combine the Philadelphia cheese with the chicken stock and onion juice.
2. Add the finely chopped cucumber and parsley.
3. Fold in the lightly whipped cream.
4. Finally, gently stir in the cooled dissolved gelatine, season to taste.
5. Turn into a wet mould, and chill until required.
6. Remove from the mould and garnish with watercress and prawns.

Cook's Note: *Use a garlic press to squeeze the juice out of the onion. A nine inch aluminium mould is ideal for this recipe- the one with the hole in the middle.*

Stuffed Lychees with Bacon

1 tin Lychees, drained
225g (8oz) streaky bacon

Stem Ginger pieces

Method

1. Pre-heat the oven to 200°C, 400°F, Gas 6.
2. Stuff the lychees with a slice of stem ginger.
3. Stretch the bacon with the back of a knife, cut into suitable strips, then roll each lychee in bacon.
4. Bake in the pre-heated oven for 6-8 minutes.Serve hot garnished with parsley.

Mozzarella, Basil and Tomato Salad

1 garlic clove, crushed
15g pack of fresh red basil leaves
30g (1oz) parmesan cheese, freshly grated
85g (3oz) pine nuts, toasted
4 tablsp olive oil
juice of half a lemon

175g (6oz) mozzarella cheese
2 ripe avocados
12 cherry tomatoes, halved
1 bag of mixed green salad leaves
Freshly ground black pepper

Method

1. Put the garlic, basil, parmesan cheese and 55g (2oz) of the pine nuts in a liquidizer and process until a thick paste is formed. Add the olive oil and lemon juice with the blades still running (take care). Spoon into the base of a large salad bowl.
2. Cut the mozzarella into rough chunks along with the avocados, toss in the salad bowl with the pesto. Gently toss the salad leaves through the pesto mixture, season with pepper.
3. Dry-fry the remaining pine nuts in a non-stick frying pan for a couple of minutes until lightly toasted, then sprinkle them over the salad and serve immediately.

Cook's Note: *Perfect for a light lunch with the girls. Serve with the bread of your choice and of course a glass of chilled white wine!*

Chicken Liver Pâté with Oatcakes and Damson Jelly

225g (8oz) chicken livers
1 small onion, chopped
2 cloves of garlic, crushed

125g (4oz) butter
300ml (10fl.oz) double cream
75ml (3fl.oz) dry sherry

Method
1. Melt 50g (2oz) of the butter in a frying pan, fry the onion for 2 minutes. Add the garlic sauté until the onion becomes opaque, remove from the pan.
2. Add the rest of the butter to the frying pan, and fry the chicken livers until soft.
3. Place all the ingredients in a blender, blend to a smooth paste. Season.
4. Turn into individual ramakins or a serving dish of your choice.
5. Serve with oatcakes and Isabella's Damson Jelly.

Oatcakes

125g (4oz) medium oatmeal
1 tablsp melted lard or dripping
pinch of bicarbonate of soda

pinch of salt
2-3 tablsp water

Method
1. Mix together the 4oz (125g) of oatmeal, dripping, bicarbonate of soda, salt and boiling water in a bowl.
2. Bring together in a ball, roll into a round, $^1/_2$ inch thick, cut into eight triangles.
3. Place on a hot girdle or hot plate, bake on one side only until the edges begin to curl, then place on a wire tray under a hot grill until they start to brown.
4. Stack in an air-tight tin. Warm through before serving, to enjoy the best flavour.

Goat's Cheese Toasts

14oz Walnut Pave loaf
375g (13oz) Goat's cheese log
Isabella's Devilish Tomato Chutney

Method
1. Pre-heat the grill.
2. Trim the ends from the loaf, and cut in half length ways.
3. Slice each half into 18, put on a baking sheet and toast on one side.
4. Spread on the other side, one to two teaspoonfuls of tomato chutney.
5. Cut the Goat's cheese on the diagonal, into $^1/_2$ cm ($^1/_4$ in) slices, place on top of the relish. Grill until the cheese is bubbling.

Cook's Note: *This is simplicity itself, and so delicious. Any type of bread may be used from the vast range available in supermarkets.*

Stuffed Red Peppers

2 large red peppers
12 cherry tomatoes
4 tablsp pine nuts
Fresh thyme

1 clove of garlic
Isabella's Devilish Tomato Chutney
4oz Scottish cheddar

Method
Pre-heat the oven to 200°C, 400°F, Gas mark 6. Slice the red peppers in half along it's length, cutting the stalk in two. De-seed the peppers, place in a roasting tin and fill each half, with 6 small cherry tomatoes cut in half, 1 tablespoon of pine nuts, some thyme leaves, $^1/_2$ clove thinly sliced garlic, and two teaspoons of Isabella's Devilish Tomato Chutney. Roast for 30-35 minutes then top each half with 25g (1oz) grated cheddar, cook for a further 10-15 minutes until golden.

Carol-Ann's Savoury Crostini's

3 anchovies, chopped
1 medium red onion, finely chopped
3 cloves of garlic, crushed
1 tsp oregano or thyme
Seasoning (salt and pepper)

18 olives, chopped
3 tomatoes, skinned and chopped
6 tsp tomato puree
3 tablsp chopped parsley
1 baguette thinly sliced

Method

1. Combine the first four ingredients. Season.
2. Mix together with all other ingredients except the baguette.
3. Set aside to allow to marinade.
4. Spread the thinly sliced crostini on a baking sheet, drizzle with olive oil, bake in a moderately hot oven, for 10-12 minutes or until lightly browned.
5. Allow to cool on a wire cooling rack.
6. To serve, pile the marinade mixture on top of the crostini, serve to guests as an appetiser.

Cook's Note: *These are delicious served with a glass of chilled white wine, as guests arrive for the evening. Both the crostini and the savoury mix can be made in advance.*

THE LIGHT BITE

Sausage and Potato Bake

1kg (2lbs) potatoes, peeled
1 tsp Worcester sauce
1 tsp tomato puree
salt and pepper

450g (1lb) sausage meat or pork
415g tin baked beans
1oz butter

Method

1. Peel and thinly slice the potatoes, place in cold water.
2. Grease a 1 litre (2pt) pie dish. Heat the oven to 180°C, 350°F, Gas Mark 4.
3. Blend the baked beans with the Worcester sauce and the tomato puree.
4. Roll the sausage meat into small balls, flatten slightly and place on top of the bean mixture.
5. Dry the sliced potatoes, arrange over the sausage meat in layers, season and dot with butter.
6. Cover the pie dish in tin foil.
7. Bake in the pre-heated oven for 30-40 minutes until golden brown.

Cook's Note: *To get a nice brown finish to the dish, place it under a hot grill before serving.*

Cherry Tomato and Basil Sauce
for pasta

The best recipes are often the simplest, and happen quite by chance. When testing recipes for Isabella's cookbook, this turned out to be a favourite, for all.

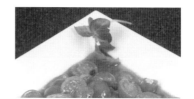

2 punnets of cherry tomatoes (about 600g/1lb5oz)
1 lemon
2 tablsp Isabella's Devilish Tomato Chutney
2 tsp sun dried tomato paste
2 cloves of garlic, crushed
a handful of basil leaves, torn
3-4 tablsp olive oil
Seasoning

Method
1. Halve the cherry tomatoes, place in a microwave bowl.
2. Add the juice of one lemon, and all other ingredients to the bowl.
3. Microwave on full for 2 minutes, stirring once during that time.
4. Allow sauce to stand for 2 minutes, check seasoning. Microwave a further 2 minutes.
5. Serve over the pasta of your choice.

Cook's Note: *This vibrant and colourful sauce could also be served with chicken or fish. Care should be taken not to over-cook the cherry tomatoes. They should have just have started to soften, but not to lose their shape.*

This recipe can be seen on page 4 of the colour section.

Spaghetti with a Chilli Tomato Sauce

2 tablsp olive oil
1 onion, finely chopped
1 clove garlic, crushed
400g (14oz) spaghetti
2 x 425g (15oz) canned chopped tomatoes
Freshly grated parmesan cheese to serve

$^1/_2$ tsp dried chilli flakes
salt and freshly ground black pepper
1 tablsp Isabella's Devilish Tomato Chutney

Method

1. Sauté the onion in one tablespoonful of oil until it is opaque in colour.
2. Add the garlic and chilli flakes, sauté for a further minute.
3. Add the chopped tomatoes and Isabella's Devilish Tomato Chutney, stir well.
4. Simmer, uncovered for 10 to 15 minutes, reducing the sauce to a thick consistency.
5. Season with salt and pepper.
6. Boil the pasta in salted water, with a tablespoonful of olive oil, added to the water.
7. Boil the pasta till al dente, drain return to the pan.
8. Divide between four pasta bowls, spoon a generous amount of sauce over the top. Pass round the parmesan cheese at the table.

Cook's Note: *This is a quick and easy Friday night special for friends. Don't forget the glass of wine !!*

Deep Pan Pizza

A Family Favourite

225g (¹/₂ lb) plain flour
1tsp cream of tartar
¹/₂ tsp bicarbonate of soda
¹/₂ tsp salt
A good pinch of cayenne pepper
1 tsp mustard powder

50g (2oz) grated cheese
60g (2¹/₂ oz) margarine
1 egg
400g (14oz) tin of tomatoes

TOPPING
2 Tablsp Isabella's Mustard Relish
25g (1oz) grated cheddar
50g (2oz) sliced salami

Method

1. Pre-heat the oven to 230°C, 450°F, Gas Mark 7. Mix all the dry ingredients together and rub in the margarine, stir in the cheese.
2. Separate the juice from the tomatoes.
3. Stir the tomato juice into the dry ingredients.
4. Bind the milk and egg, add to the mixture to form a firm dough.
5. Roll out the dough to 1" thick.
6. Place on a baking tray, which has been lined with tinfoil, and brushed with oil.
   Line the baking tray with the dough.
7. Scatter the chopped tomatoes and salami over the top.
8. Mix the mustard relish with the cheese sprinkle over the top.
9. Bake for 25-30 minutes

Cook's Note: *Serve with salad. The pizza freezes well.*

Savoury Chicken Drum sticks

8 Chicken drum sticks
2 tablsp soy sauce
$^1/_2$ pint (8fl.oz) chicken stock
2 tsp curry powder
2 tsp Worcester sauce

2 tsp vinegar
2 tsp Isabella's Tomato Chutney
2 tsp Isabella's Mustard Relish
2 tsp demerara sugar

Method

1. Score the chicken drum sticks diagonally with a sharp knife.Set aside.
2. Place all other ingredients in a sauce pan, bring to the boil, reduce quantity by half.
3. Pour the marinade over the drum sticks, (set aside for a least 20 minutes, preferably overnight).
4. Heat the oven to 400°F, 200°C, Gas Mark 6. Bake the chicken drum sticks and marinade for around 20 minutes, basting the drum sticks twice during the cooking process.

Cook's Note: *This is a wonderful supper recipe for children and adults alike.*

Tomato and Basil Tarts

1 tablsp olive oil
2 cloves garlic, crushed
2 handfuls, of fresh basil
125g (40oz) finely chopped shallots
8-10 large tomatoes, chopped
50g (2oz) freshly grated parmesan
450g (1lb) puff pastry

Method

1. Pre-heat the oven to 220°C, 425°F, Gas 7.
2. Roll the puff pastry out to $\frac{1}{8}$th of an inch thick. Cut into $2\frac{1}{2}''$ rounds.
3. Place on a baking sheet, prick the centre lightly with a fork. Chill.
4. Sauté the finely chopped shallots and garlic until opaque
5. Add the chopped tomatoes, 25g (1oz) of the parmesan, and a handful of basil leaves.
6. Season well.
7. Spread the tomato mixture over the pastry leaving a $\frac{1}{2}$ inch border. Brush with beaten egg. Bake for 20-30 minutes, or until well risen and brown.
8. Serve immediately.

Cook's Note: *A fluted cutter gives a nice finish to the pastry.*

Bacon, Avocado
and Pecan Salad

250g (8oz) back bacon (cut in small strips)
250g (8oz) baby leaf spinach
2 medium avocados, sliced

2 shallots, finely chopped
125g (4oz) cherry tomatoes, halved
100g (4oz) pecan nuts, roughly chopped

The Dressing

2 tablsp olive oil
2 tablsp Isabella's Devilish Tomato Chutney
Salt and Pepper

1 tablsp red wine vinegar
a pinch of mustard powder

Method

1. Dry fry the bacon and shallots in a frying pan over a medium heat until golden. This will take about 5 minutes. Set aside.
2. Meanwhile, heat the oven to 200°C, 400°F, Gas mark 6.
3. Place the pecans on a baking sheet, bake for 2-3 minutes in the hot oven, set aside to cool.
4. Combine all the ingredients for the dressing except the seasoning, shake well, season to taste.
5. Combine the baby spinach leaves, cherry tomatoes and avocados in a salad bowl.
6. Tip the bacon, pecan nuts and dressing over the salad and serve.

Cook's Note: *This could be used as a starter or a main course side salad, for four people.*

FISHY BUSINESS

Arbroath Smokie Flan

2 Smokies skinned and boned
8fl.oz. ($^1/_2$ pint) double cream
2 eggs

For the pastry:
225g (8oz) plain flour
125g (4oz) butter, cubed

1 egg yolk
Ground pepper
Grated nutmeg

Cold water for mixing
Pinch salt

Method
1. Pre-heat the oven to 220°C, 425°F, Gas 7.
2. Grease a 25cm x 3.25cm deep (9$^3/_4$ x 1$^1/_4$ inch) deep flan tin with a removable base.
3. In a mixing bowl, sieve the flour, add the butter and rub into the flour until the mixture resembles fine breadcrumbs.
4. Add the cold water by the tablespoon, using a broad bladed knife to bring the pastry together, to form a ball. Turn on to a floured board. Knead lightly. Wrap in cling film and chill for thirty minutes.
5. Roll out and line the tart tin. Line the pastry base and sides with greaseproof paper, and fill with dry beans or rice. Bake blind for 18-20 minutes or until the pastry is set. Remove from the oven, take out the greaseproof and beans. Return to the oven for a further 10 minutes or until crisp. Turn the oven down to 180°C, 350°F, Gas 4.
6. To make the filling: Line the base of the cooked tart tin with the prepared smokies.
7. Beat the eggs and egg yolk together, whisk together with the cream, season with ground pepper and add some freshly grated nutmeg. Pour over the pastry base and bake for 25-30 minutes or until the custard is set.
   Serve warm with a leafy green salad and baked potato.

Cook's Note: *These can be served as 4 individual tartlets as seen on page 2 of the colour section. If the pastry base is cracked, brush with beaten egg yolk to create a seal and prevent leakage.*

Pasta with Smoked Salmon

1½ pints of thin cheese sauce
110g (4oz) tri-coloured pasta, cooked
2 tablsp Isabella's Dill Mustard Relish
75g (3oz) smoked salmon, cut in strips
75g (3oz) grated mature cheddar

Method

1. Mix a tablespoonful of Isabella's Dill Mustard Relish into the cheese sauce.
2. Stir in the cooked pasta and smoked salmon.
3. Turn into a greased oven proof dish.
4. Mix the grated cheese with the remainder of the mustard relish. Sprinkle on top and place under a hot grill until brown and crisp.
5. Serve immediately with a green salad and crispy french bread.

Cook's Note: *This dish can be made ahead and frozen, or stored overnight in the refrigerator. A thinner cheese sauce is not absorbed by the pasta as much, otherwise the consistency of the dish is too thick.*

Marinated Mustard Trout

4 fillets of trout skinned and cut diagonally

FOR THE MARINADE

2fl.oz (80mls) wine vinegar
juice and rind of one lemon
1 tablsp Isabella's Mustard Relish

2fl.oz (80mls) water
1 tablsp chopped parsley
1 tsp honey

FOR THE DRESSING

1 tablsp wine vinegar
1 tsp honey
1 tablsp Isabella's Mustard Relish
Seasoning to taste

1 tsp lemon juice
2 tablsp olive oil
1 tablsp chopped parsley

Method

1. Mix all the ingredients for the marinade together, shake well. Pour over the filleted trout.
2. Chill overnight.
3. Remove the trout from the marinade, discard the marinade.
4. Serve on a bed of chiffonade lettuce, passing the dressing around in a sauce boat.

Cook's Note: *This makes a nice summer supper dish for family and friends*

Grilled Tuna with Tomato Sauce

4 tuna steaks 225g (8oz) each in weight
3 garlic cloves, crushed
1 medium onion, chopped
Dash of white wine
Seasoning

3 tablsp olive oil
450g (1lb) of ripe tomatoes, chopped
1 tablsp tomato puree
3-4 tablsp Isabella's Devilish Tomato
Chutney

Method

1. Heat 2 tablespoonfuls of oil in a saucepan, add the onion and garlic, sauté until opaque.
2. Add the chopped tomatoes, tomato puree, Isabella's Devilish Tomato Chutney and a dash of
   white wine, simmer uncovered for 20 minutes. Check the seasoning.
3. Tip into the food processor, blend to a smooth consistency.
4. Set aside.
5. Heat a chargrill pan until hot. Brush the tuna steaks with the remaining oil.
6. Cook for 2 minutes, then turn clockwise to get the markings from the grill pan,
   giving a criss cross effect on the steaks, cook a further 1-2 minutes.
7. Turn the fish over and repeat the process.
8. Serve with baked potatoes, green beans and garden peas. The sauce can be passed
   around for anyone who wishes.

Cooks Note: *Serve with a crisp green salad and Italian bread to mop up the juices.*

Stir Fried Prawns with Mint and Mustard

Gillian who works with us at Isabella's Preserves, loved this recipe when we were recipe testing. We hope you enjoy it too.

4 tablsp olive oil (mild flavoured)
2 hot dried red chillies
1 tablsp freshly chopped coriander
450g (1lb) medium sized raw prawns
225g (8oz) small prawns, raw
Wedges of lime

2 tsp Isabella's Mustard Relish
3-4 cloves garlic, crushed
1 tablsp freshly chopped mint
Seasoning

Method

1. Peel and de-vein the prawns leaving the tails on, rinse and pat them dry, chill until required.
2. Heat the oil to a high temperature in a wok or heavy based frying pan.
3. Add the mustard seeds and roughly broken chillies, when the mustard seeds begin to pop add the garlic, stir fry for a further 2-3 minutes.
4. Add the prawns. Continue stir frying the prawns, until they are opaque in colour. Season to taste.
5. Add the fresh coriander and mint.
5. Serve over plain boiled rice, with some nan bread and lime wedges for passing.

Cook's Note: *This is a hot, spicy dish with subtle flavours. The prawns make it that bit extra special, King Prawns are scrummy but expensive, but for the special occasion, go for it!!*

Prawn Curry
with
pilau rice and nan bread

600g (1lb 5oz) frozen prawns
1 onion, finely chopped
125g (4oz) mangetout, sliced lenghthways
1 jar of Isabella's Hot Banana Chutney
1 tablsp ground nut oil

4 cooked medium prawns for decoration
2 Bird's Eye Chillies, finely chopped
2 tablsp coriander, chopped
8fl.oz (250mls) half fat coconut milk

Method

1. Heat the oil in a large non-stick frying pan or wok.
2. Sauté the onion, until opaque in colour, add the chilli's, stir fry a further minute.
3. Add the whole jar of Hot Banana Chutney and the coconut milk.
4. Bring to the boil, then simmer gently, adding the mangetout followed by the prawns a few minutes later.
5. Stir in the coriander, season to taste.
6. Serve immediately with pilau rice and nan bread. The cooked prawns for decoration should be peeled, with the tails left on, washed and gently dried.

Cook's Note: *It is very easy to over-cook prawns whether frozen or fresh, fresh prawns should turn opaque when cooked. Frozen prawns should be de-frosted thoroughly before use, rinsed and cooked enough to heat them through, a few minutes is sufficient.*

Thai Crab Cakes
with a
Chilli Dipping Sauce

3 tablsp olive oil
2 sticks of celery, chopped finely
2 Bird's Eye Chilli's, chopped
1 egg beaten
225g (8oz) fresh bread crumbs
Fresh white bread crumbs for coating

1 red bell pepper, chopped finely
2 red onions, chopped, finely
2 tins white crab meat, drained
1 tablsp Devilish Tomato Chutney
Seasoning

For the chilli sauce:

1x 2.5ml(½ tsp) finely chopped root ginger
2x 5ml (2 tsp) brown sugar
1x 15ml (1 tablsp) dry sherry

½ mild red chilli
1x 2.5 ml (½ tsp) light soy sauce

Method
1. Heat the oil in a heavy based frying pan. Sauté the red onions for a few minutes. Add the celery, bell pepper and chilli, sauté gently until all the vegetables are tender. This will take 5-7 minutes. Add the Devilish Tomato Chutney, and seasoning, stir well.
2. Add the drained white crab meat,and bread crumbs, bind with the beaten egg.
3. Make into 16 small crab cakes coating with bread crumbs, flatten out slightly on a tray and refrigerate, overnight if possible.
4. Fry the crab cakes 3 minutes each side or until firm.
5. Blend all ingredients for the sauce in the food processor. Pass around the table, as dipping sauce for the fish cakes.

Cook's Note: *Serve with a salad garnish of carrots, spring onions and cucumber cut in strips strips, and some lime wedges.*

Smoked Mackeral
with a
Potato, Horseradish Salad

450g (1lb) new potatoes
2 tablsp half fat crème fraîche, or cream
4 tablsp olive oil
2 fillets of smoked mackeral
100g bag of watercress or preferred salad leaves

1 tablsp lemon juice
2 crisp apples
2 tablsp Isabella's Horseradish Sauce

Method

1. Cook the potatoes in boiling salted water for 15-20 minutes or until tender.
   Drain and set aside.
2. In a bowl mix the horseradish sauce, crème fraîche, lemon juice, olive oil and seasoning.
3. Remove the core from the apples leaving on the skin, cut into bite size chunks, mix with
   the warm potatoes.
4. Skin and flake the smoked mackeral, add to the bowl, gently combine all ingredients, check
   the seasoning.
5. Add the watercress or mixed salad leaves toss lightly, serve immediately.

Cook's Note: *This unusual salad is a great lunch time special, served with warm bread rolls,*
or ciabatta it will go down a treat.

Smoked Salmon Tartlets

225g (8oz) plain flour
120g (4oz) butter

Pinch of salt
Cold water

<u>Filling</u>:

10oz smoked salmon trimmings
5fl.oz. crème fraîche
2 tsp Isabella's Mustard Relish
Seasoning

2 eggs
1 egg yolk
1 tablsp chopped parsley

Method

1. Blend the flour, butter, and pinch of salt in a food processor. Add the cold water a little at a time, until the mixture forms a ball. Wrap in cling film and chill for 30 minutes.
2. Roll the pastry out to $\frac{1}{8}$ th of an inch thick. Cut out as many rounds as possible with a fluted $2\frac{1}{2}''$ cutter. Press into a patty tin, chill.
3. Chop the smoked salmon trimmings, fill the pastry cases.
4. Combine the crème fraîche, eggs, mustard relish, chopped parsley and seasoning.
5. Pour into the pastry cases.
6. Bake in a hot oven. 200°C, 400°F Gas 6 for 15-20 minutes or until well risen and brown on top.
7. Serve warm.

Cook's Note: *Serve these to guests with a glass of chilled white wine, when they arrive for dinner.*

Tangy Shrimp
on
the Grill

50g (2oz) unsalted butter
1 tsp cayenne pepper
125mls (4fl.oz) dry white wine
450g (1lb) jumbo shrimp (roughly 16)

1 tablsp finely chopped garlic
2 tsp Isabella's Devilish Tomato
Chutney

Method

1. Pre-heat the barbecue to a high temperature.
2. De-vein the shrimp, but do not peel them, chill until required.
3. In a small saucepan over a medium heat, combine butter, garlic and cayenne pepper.
4. Sauté until the garlic is soft, this will take about 5 minutes, stir in the tomato chutney.
5. Add the wine and raise the heat, reduce the quantity of the marinade by half.
6. Pour over the shrimp marinade at least 20 minutes.
7. Place the shrimp directly over the high heat and grill, turning only once.
8. When the shrimp turn opaque in colour they are cooked, this will take approximately 3-4 minutes. Serve immediately, with plenty of paper napkins to mop up the juices.

Cook's Note: *An expensive treat, but for a special occasion, it is a great recipe which can be served with so many different complimentary dishes. Baby new potatoes in a herb butter is a great accompaniment. Cook them on the grill top for 20-25 minutes.*

Whole Side of Salmon
with
Brown Sugar and Mustard Glaze

25g (1oz) unsalted butter
1 tsp honey
1 tablsp light soy sauce
2 tsp grated ginger
1 whole salmon fillet, skin on, ¾ to 1 inch thick

25g (1oz) brown sugar
1 tablsp Isabella's Mustard Relish
1 tablsp olive oil

Method

1. Prepare the barbecue. The grill should be pre-heated to medium hot.
2. In a small sauté pan, melt the butter, add the brown sugar and honey, stir well until combined.
3. Remove from the heat, and whisk in the mustard, soy sauce, olive oil and ginger, cool.
4. Place the salmon skin side down a large sheet of aluminium foil. Leave a border of 2 inches around the fish.
5. Brush the cooled marinade over the salmon. Place on a prepared medium hot grill, brush with marinade three to four times during cooking.
6. The cooking time is approximately 20-25 minutes. The edges of the salmon should be brown, and the inside opaque in colour.
7. Transfer the salmon on the foil to a cutting board.
8. Serve in six to eight pieces leaving the skin intact. Slide a spatula between the skin and flesh, and remove the salmon pieces to a serving platter.

Cook's Note: *The barbecue has become a very useful resource for the busy lifestyle. It is fun for all, especially the dad's standing cooking under an umbrella in the rain. We do love our Scottish Harr and misty rain, it's all part of the Scottish character!!*

ON THE MAIN

Pork Chops with Orange Sauce

50g (2oz) unsalted butter
4 boneless pork chops
4 tablsp (60mls) Isabella's Seville Orange Marmalade
5 fl.oz ($\frac{1}{4}$ pt) white wine
5 fl.oz ($\frac{1}{4}$ pt) double cream
1 tablsp freshly chopped parsley

Method

1. Melt the butter in a heavy based frying pan, just when it starts to brown, add the chops. Brown quickly on both sides. Remove from the pan and keep warm.
2. Pour the white wine into the hot frying pan, let the wine come quickly to the boil, stirring all the time, and scraping the bottom of the pan.
3. Add the Seville Orange Marmalade, stir for one minute, bringing back to the boil. Add the orange juice and double cream.
4. Simmer for 3 minutes, check seasoning
5. Add the chops to the sauce, cook a further 10 minutes or until the pork chops are cooked through. Sprinkle over parsley. Serve.

Cook's Note: *Serve with baby new potatoes, mangetout and an avocado, watercress and orange salad on the side.*

Rack of Perthshire Lamb
with Devilled Kidneys

Recipe from Andrew Hamer, Executive Head Chef, Gleneagles Hotel

Lamb

2 x 800g boned racks of lamb
2 whole lamb kidneys
225g (8oz) sweetbreads
200g (7oz) bread crumbs
Dijon mustard

Method

Remove lamb loin from the racks. Remove any sinew. Sear off in a hot pan.
Place in a hot oven for 6-10 minutes.
Remove the sinews from the kidneys and sweetbreads by placing in boiling water then plunging in cold water. Cut into slices.

Herb Crust

175g (6oz) brioche bread crumbs
50g (2oz) tarragon
$^1/_2$ clove of garlic
salt and pepper
200g (7oz) parsley
50g (2oz) spinach
50g (2oz) Dijon mustard

Method

Blend the parsley, tarragon, spinach and garlic to form green herb crumbs.
Smear one side of the cooked lamb with a little Dijon mustard and roll in the bread crumbs.
Place under the grill to crispen slightly.

Fondant Potato
4 Baking Potatoes
200ml clarified butter
5g thyme
30g (1^1/$_2$oz) diced butter
28g rock salt
small clove garlic
5ml (1tsp) oil
200ml white chicken stock

Method
Seal the potatoes in clarified butter and oil. Add the rock salt, garlic, thyme, diced butter and chicken stock. Cook in a moderate oven, 180°C until golden brown.

Sauce

Bones from racks of lamb
6 peppercorns
1ltr lamb stock
200mls dark port
50g soft dice butter
Mirepoix of vegetables (carrots, onion, celery and leek)

5 cloves of garlic
2 bay leaves
1 dsp Isabella's Damson Jelly
2^1/$_2$ sprigs of rosemary

Method
Sweat off chopped up bones and mixed vegetables, peppercorn, bay leaf and garlic. Add Isabella's Damson jelly, then the lamb stock. Reduce by ^{2}/$_3$ to coating consistency. Pass through a sieve. Adjust seasoning.

To Serve
Place the fondant potato on the plate, then the sweetbread with the lamb placed on top, with the kidney at the other side.
Spoon the sauce around the plate.

Marinated, Chargrilled Lemon and Lime Chicken Fillets

4 chicken breasts
2 tablsp Isabella's Lemon and Lime Marmalade
50g (2oz) butter

Method

1. Place the chicken fillets in a polybag, place them flat on a chopping board. Beat them until flat with a rolling pin.
2. Put them into a plastic box and toss them in Isabella's Lemon and Lime Marmalade and cover.
3. Place in the fridge to marinade for at least one hour, overnight is preferable.
2. Melt the rest of the butter in a frying pan (it should be very hot), brown the chicken fillets on both sides. This will take 2-4 minutes each side. Check to see if the chicken juices run clear.

Cook's Note: *Serve with baked potatoes and a green salad.*

Meat Loaf

1 egg
1 medium onion
4 tablsp Worcester sauce
1 tsp (5ml) mustard powder
450g (1lb) steak mince

100g (4oz) smoked bacon
1 clove garlic, crushed
1 tablsp tomato puree
1½ tsp (7.5ml) salt
125g (4oz) brown bread crumbs

Method

1. Heat the oven to 350°F, 180°C, Gas Mark 4.
2. Combine all the ingredients in a blender except the bread crumbs and steak mince. Blend well.
3. Place in a bowl and then mix the mince and bread crumbs in by hand.
4. Line a 1lb loaf tin with aluminium foil, grease the foil, tip in the meat loaf mixture.
5. Bake on the centre shelf of the oven for about 1-1½ hours.

Cook's Note: *Serve hot with potatoes and a green vegetable, or cold with a salad. This is one of my daughter Isabella's favourite recipes.*

Crown of Lamb with Herb Stuffing and Roasted New Potatoes

Asking the local butcher to prepare a crown of lamb for you takes so much of the worry out of preparing the dish.

Allow 2-3 cutlets for each person.

<u>2 Racks of Lamb</u>

<u>Herb Stuffing</u>

300g (10oz) bread crumbs	3 egg yolks
75g (3oz) melted butter	2 sprigs rosemary, chopped
2 sprigs thyme, chopped	seasoning

Method

1. Heat the oven to 450°F, 230°C, Gas Mark 8. Place the oven shelf, second from the bottom.
2. Place all the dry ingredients for the stuffing in a bowl, pour in the melted butter, mix together, combine with the egg yolks.
3. Place the lamb in a roasting tin. Spoon into the centre of the crown of lamb.
4. Roast for 30-45 minutes depending on the size of the crown.

<u>Roasted New Potatoes</u>

1kg (2lbs) new potatoes
4 tablsp olive oil
rock salt
Thinly slice the potatoes the potatoes, but not all the way through. Leave in cold water for 1 hour. Drain. Pre-heat the oil in a roasting tin when the oil is smoking hot, add the potatoes, and sprinkle with rock salt. Baste occasionally. Cook until crisp, serve with the lamb.

To Serve: Place the crown on a large serving plate or ashet. Carve at the dining table, giving 2 cutlets per person.

Medallions of Venison
in
Damson Jelly with Gin Sauce

Your local butcher is the best person to get advice on the required cut of venison. However our supermarkets now provide an extensive range of game products of our choice.

4 fillets venison
75g (3oz) butter
seasoning
2 tablsp (30ml) Isabella's Damson Jelly with Gin
10 fl.oz beef stock
5 fl.oz red wine

Method

1. Melt the butter in a large frying pan, until "smoking" hot.
2. Fry off the venison fillets on both sides, until just pink in the middle. This takes 2-3 minutes.
3. Remove from the pan and keep warm.
4. Add the stock and red wine to the hot frying pan, de-glaze the pan, reducing the liquid to half quantity.
5. Add the Damson Jelly, stir to dissolve in the sauce.
6. Adjust the seasoning to taste.
7. Pour over the venison fillets. Serve.

Cook's Note: *Creamed potatoes and French green beans would compliment this dish well.*

Stuffed Pork Fillet
wrapped in Filo Pastry

Get the local butcher to split the pork fillet and flatten it for you. It makes it far easier to stuff, and roll up.

1 pork fillet
1 package filo pastry (defrosted)
125g (4oz) butter
1 onion (finely chopped)
50g (2oz) dried prunes (finely chopped)
50g (2oz) dried apricots (finely chopped)
50g (2oz) pine nuts
75g (3oz) bread crumbs
juice of $\frac{1}{2}$ lemon
$\frac{1}{2}$ beaten egg
2 tablsp chopped parsley

Method

1. Pre-heat the oven to 200°C, 400°F. Gas 6.
2. De-frost the filo pastry.
3. Melt 50g (2oz) butter in a heavy based frying pan, add the onion and celery sauté until opaque in colour, or soft, add the prunes, apricots, bread crumbs and lemon juice.
4. Bind with beaten egg.
5. Lay out the pork fillet flat, spread the stuffing over, roll up tightly. Place the fillet on cling film, wrap and twist the ends tightly, chill.
6. Lay the filo pastry out flat, cover with a damp tea towel.
7. Melt the remainder of the butter.
8. Brush four sheets of filo with butter, layering one on top of the other.
9. Unwrap the fillet, place in the centre of the filo, wrap up like a parcel, bring all ends folded to the top, brush with butter.

Pork Fillet Wrapped in Filo Pastry continued from page 46

10. Brush individual sheets of filo, tearing them into strips and scrunching them with your fingers, cover the top and sides of the filo, this may seem a strange thing to do, but it looks great once cooked.
11. Transfer to a baking tray using a fish slice, bake for 20 minutes at 400°F, 200°C, Gas 6, then turn the oven down to 375°F, 180°C, Gas Mark 4.
12. Bake for a further 30 minutes to ensure the fillet is cooked throughout. The pastry should be golden brown.

Cook's Note: *Cover the pastry in grease proof paper, which is crumpled and dampened with water, if it is getting too brown.*
Use an electric knife to cut into slices for serving - it's a lot easier!!

Duck Breast
with
Wild Cherry and Bramble Sauce

4 duck breasts with the skin on, prick the skin with a fork

10 fl.oz ('/₂ pint) chicken stock
40g (1'/₂oz) unsalted butter
75g (3oz) pecan nuts
seasoning

60mls (4 tablsp) Sloe Liqueur
30mls (2 tablsp) double cream
2 tablsp Wild Cherry & Bramble Sauce

Method

1. Pre-heat the oven to 180°C, 375°F, Gas Mark 4. Melt the butter in a heavy based frying pan.
2. When the butter is just beginning to brown, add the duck breasts skin side down. Sear on both sides, remove to an oven proof dish.
3. Place in the pre-heated oven for approximately 10 minutes, until the duck is just still pink in the middle.
4. Break up the pecans using your fingers, roast on a baking tray in a moderately hot oven for 3-4 minutes.
5. Meanwhile, de-glaze the frying pan with the sloe liqueur, adding the chicken stock. Reduce the quantity by one third.
6. Add the Wild Cherry and Bramble Sauce and double cream, simmer to desired consistency. Season to taste.
7. Add the pecans and combine well.
8. Serve over the duck breast, which has been sliced using an electric knife and fanned over one side of the plate.

Cook's Note: *Serve with rosti potatoes or daphinoise, and a green vegetable of your choice.*

Casserole of Scotch Beef

4 tablsp olive oil
1½ kg (3lb) stewing steak
5 cloves garlic, crushed
2 tablsp flour

1 bottle fruity young claret
salt and freshly ground black pepper
1 tsp sugar
a bunch of fresh herbs

Method
Pre-heat the oven to 150°C 300°F Gas 2.
Cut the meat into 4cm (1½") cubes. Heat the oil in a heavy based, deep casserole dish.
Brown the meat in batches, return all the meat to the casserole. Add the garlic and
sprinkle in the flour leave uncovered over a low heat and continue browning for a further 15
minutes, stirring frequently. Add the wine and herbs, season.
Cover and simmer for 3 hours in the oven until the meat is tender. Remove from the oven and
stir in the vegetable trimmings. Heat through, stir in finely chopped parsley.

The Vegetable Trimmings

150g (5oz) lean bacon
6-8 very small onions

125g (4oz) button mushrooms

Method
Cook the bacon in an enamelled cast-iron frying pan till lightly browned, add the onions and
cook for about 10 minutes. Remove the mushroom stalks add them to the pan, stir, cover and
cook gently for a further 10 minutes. Set aside until ready to add the the meat.

Cook's Note: *The type of wine used in this recipe depends on the individual taste. A*
Burgundy or Beaujolais would do very nicely, and can be polished off at the
table.

Savoury Stuffed Pancakes
with a
Chicken and Hot Banana Sauce

Veronica who works with us at Isabella's Preserves gave me this recipe for the cookbook, it turned out to be quite a hit, with everyone.

<u>Pancake Recipe</u>

125g (4oz) plain flour
pinch of salt
1 egg, lightly beaten
300mls (½ pint) milk
oil or butter for frying

Method

1. An 18cm (7″) pancake pan or heavy based frying pan is suitable for this recipe.
2. Use a light vegetable oil or butter for greasing the pan.
3. Whiz all ingredients in the food processor, tip into a jug. Rest for 30 minutes.
4. Put a little oil or butter in the pan and heat until it starts to smoke, pour off any excess oil.
5. Pour in a little batter, tilting the pan until the base is coated in a thin layer.
6. Cook for 1-2 minutes, until the underside is golden.
7. Flip the pancake over with a palette knife, and cook for a further 30-45 seconds, until it is an even golden colour.
8. Slide the pancake on to a cooling rack. Use a tea towel to slip the pancakes inside of to keep them warm.

Savoury Stuffed Pancakes with a Chicken, Hot Banana Sauce
continued from page 50

Chicken and Hot Banana Sauce

3 chicken breasts
1 jar of Isabella's Hot Banana Chutney
$^1/_2$ tin half fat coconut milk
8fl.oz. ($^1/_2$ pnt) chicken stock

Method

1. Pre-heat the oven to 400°F, 200°C, Gas Mark 6.
2. Sear the chicken breasts in hot butter. Place in the pre-heated oven for 10 minutes further cooking.
3. Meanwhile de-glaze the frying pan with half a pint of chicken stock, reducing to $^1/_3$ of the quantity.
4. Add Isabella's Hot Banana Chutney.
5. Pour in the coconut milk, and simmer gently.
6. Cut the chicken breast into bite sized chunks. Combine with the sauce, check the seasoning.
7. Roll two tablespoonfuls of sauce into each pancake. Serve each person two pancakes, with a crispy green leaf salad and mangetout.

Cook's Note: *The pancakes can be made and frozen or kept in the refrigerator.*

Special Shepherd's Pie

700g (1½ lb) lamb, coarsely minced
2 tablsp cooking oil
3 onions, finely chopped
3 carrots, cut into fine dice
1 tablsp tomato puree
200mls (7fl.oz) beef stock
Seasoning

½ tsp ground cumin
½ tsp fresh thyme, chopped
½ tsp fresh rosemary, chopped
2 glasses red wine
1oz plain flour
2 tsp Worcester sauce
1kg (2lbs) mashed potato

Method

1. Sear the minced lamb at a high temperature to seal in the juices.
2. Add the chopped vegetables and herbs.
3. Allow to cook for 5-6 minutes, adding the tomato puree and Worcester sauce.
4. Add the wine in two batches, reducing the quantity between each addition.
5. Sprinkle the flour into the pan and cook for 2-3 minutes.
6. Pour in the stock and gently simmer for 1½ - 2 hours.
7. During this time boil and mash the potatoes, stir in a knob of butter and some milk.
8. Place the minced lamb sauce in an oven proof casserole, top with the mashed potato.
9. Finish in a hot oven, 200°C, 400°F, Gas Mark 5 for 30-40 minutes.

Cook's Note: *Serve with garden peas or green salad.*

Prime Beef Burgers

1kg (2lbs) minced beef
2 medium onions, chopped
2 tablsp cooking oil
225g (8oz) white breadcrumbs

1 dessert spoon tomato puree
2 tablsp freshly cut mixed herbs
2 eggs beaten
Salt and pepper

Method

1. In a frying pan sauté the onion until opaque in colour, cool on a plate.
2. Place all other ingredients in a mixing bowl, adding the cooled onion. Mix well.
3. Chill for 1 hour. Form into hamburger patties with wet hands, this should make 8 large ham burgers.
4. Either barbecue, or grill on a hot grill plate to the required taste.

Serve with:
Easy Barbecue Sauce and Isabella's Devilish Tomato Chutney

60 ml Sunflower oil
250g (8oz) finely chopped onion
120mls water
125g (4oz) brown sugar
Salt to taste

120mls lemon juice
45mls Worcester sauce
30ml Isabella's Mustard Relish
250g (8oz) Isabella's Devilish Tomato Sauce
$\frac{1}{4}$ tsp freshly ground pepper

Place all the ingredients in a microwave safe bowl. Cook on full power until boiling, for 10 minutes. (Based on a 900w microwave oven)

FOR THE SWEET TOOTH

Strawberry, Apricot and Tangerine Pavlova

6 egg whites
350g (12oz) castor sugar
$^1/_2$ tsp Rose Water
3 tablsp Isabella's Apricot & Tangerine Conserve
20 fl.oz ($^1/_2$ pt) double cream
1 package fresh strawberries
mint leaves for decoration

Method

1. Heat the oven to 150°C, 300°F, Gas Mark 3.
2. Cover a baking sheet with grease proof paper.
3. Place the egg white in a large baking bowl, whisk using an electric whisk, until stiff. Add the castor sugar gradually, beating between additions. Fold in the Rose Water.
4. Spoon onto the grease-proof paper, making two rounds, and bake for 1 - 1$^1/_2$ hours. Cool.
5. Beat the cream till it holds its shape, fold in the, and conserve. Slice half the strawberries, fold into the cream mixture.
6. Spoon the cream mixture over the meringue base.
7. Place the second meringue round on top.
8. Decorate with whole and sliced strawberries, some blobs of cream and Apricot & Tangerine Conserve.
9. Finish with sprigs of mint, dust with icing sugar.

Cook's Note: *The meringue can be made well in advance, and stored in an air-tight container. This looks as good as it tastes. Featured on front cover.*

(Front Cover Recipe)

Mint Sorbet
with
Fresh Strawberries

2 egg whites
Isabella's Mint Jelly x1 jar
A few drops of green colouring
1 punnet fresh strawberries
Sprigs of fresh mint, chopped

Method

1. Beat the egg whites till stiff in the food processor.
2. Then beat in the whole jar of mint jelly.
3. Add a few drops of green colouring.
4. Turn into a plastic container and freeze.
5. Slice half of the strawberries, leave the rest whole.
6. Serve the sorbet into tall sundae glasses, and decorate with sliced and whole strawberries. Decorate with a spring of fresh mint.

Cook's Note: *This is a low fat dessert!*

Pear and Frangipane Tart

For the Sweet Pastry

175g (6oz) unsalted butter
pinch of salt
1 egg yolk

50g (2oz) castor sugar
250g (8oz) plain flour
1 tablsp cold water

Method

Whiz all ingredients in the food processor, until they form a ball. Tip onto a clean work surface, knead lightly. Wrap in cling film, chill for 30 minutes. Roll out to line a loose based 25cm flan ring, prick the base of the tart with a fork, chill.

For the Almond Cream

100g (3½oz) butter, softened
100g (3½oz) castor sugar
100g (3½oz) ground almonds
3 medium pears
150mls Isabella's Apricot & Tangerine Conserve

25g (1oz) flour
1 large egg, beaten
1 egg yolk

Method

Pre-heat the oven to 400°F, 200°C, Gas Mark 5. Cream the butter and sugar until pale and light. Gradually beat in the egg and yolk, fold in the ground almonds and flour. Spoon into the chilled pastry case, spreading over the base. Peel, core and halve the pears, place 1 tsp of the conserve in each half. Push the pear halves down into the almond cream, rounded ends uppermost. Bake in the hot pre-heated oven for 10-15 minutes, then turn the heat down to 180°C, 350°F, Gas Mark 4. Continue baking for 15-20 minutes, until the almond cream is set.

Cook's Note: *Makes one 25cm tart. Serve with whipped cream or Greak yogurt.*

Lemon Soufflé

My Sister Sheila's Recipe

4 eggs
125g (4oz) castor sugar
The rind and juice of 4 lemons
1$\frac{1}{2}$ sachets of gelatine
10 fl.oz ($\frac{1}{2}$ pint) double cream

Method

1. Separate the egg whites from the yolks. Place in two separate bowls.
2. Scatter the gelatine powder over the lemon juice, dissolve by standing in a pan of warm water.
3. Beat the egg yolks and sugar together until thick and creamy.
4. Beat the egg whites until stiff.
5. Fold one tablespoonful of egg yolk mixture into the egg whites, then fold in the rest.
6. Fold in the cream, which has been lightly whipped.
7. Pour into the serving bowl.

Cook's Note: *Serve with shortbread fingers (see page 74)*

Raspberry Jam Roly Poly

For the Suet crust Pastry
200g (7oz) self raising flour
2.5ml ($^1/_2$ tsp) salt
100g (4oz) suet
about 120mls (8 tablsp) water

4-5 tablsp Isabella's Raspberry Jam

Method

1. Pre-heat the oven to 180°C, 375°F, Gas Mark 4. Grease a 33x23cm (13x9″) baking tin.
2. To make the pastry - mix the flour, salt and suet, add enough cold water to make an elastic dough. Knead lightly until smooth.
3. Roll out on a lightly floured surface, to fit a 25x23cm (11x9″) oblong baking tray. Spread the jam over the pastry, leaving a 0.5cm ($^1/_4$″) edge.
4. Brush the edges with milk, and roll the pastry, starting from a short side.
5. Lift the roll, with a fish slice on to the prepared baking tin. Bake for 40-50 minutes, until well risen and firm to touch.

Cook's Note: *Serve with hot custard or pouring cream.*

Chocolate Bread and Butter Pudding

4 slices brown bread
5 slices of fruit loaf
150g (5oz) dark chocolate
15 fl.oz (425ml) whipping cream
4oz (110g) castor sugar

3oz (75g) butter
3 large eggs
Isabella's Strawberry Jam
4 tablsp Port

Method

1. Remove the crusts from the bread, butter and spread with jam, cut into triangles.
2. Put the chocolate, whipping cream, sugar and the rest of the butter in a bowl.
3. Place in the microwave, melt and combine all ingredients.
4. Whisk the whole eggs and add to the chocolate mixture, stirring well.
5. Pour enough chocolate mixture over the base of an oven proof dish, to cover it.
6. Arrange the bread triangles over this.
7. Pour over the rest of the chocolate mixture.
8. Allow to become completely cold. Refrigerate overnight.
9. Bake in a moderate oven 180°C, 375°F, Gas Mark 6 for 30-35 minutes. Leave to stand for 10 minutes before serving.

Cook's Note: *Just go completely overboard on the calories and serve with ice-cream or double cream.*

Marshmallow Cheesecake

This extremely delicious cheesecake was given to me by Shonadh, who works with us at Isabella's Preserves, it really is worth a try!!

75g (3oz) butter, melted
150g (6oz) digestives, crushed
11g (0.4oz) sachet gelatine
1 bag American mini marshmallows
150g (6oz) cream cheese
250g (8oz) tub mascarpone cheese
284ml crème fraîche
397g can of condensed milk
90ml (6 tablsp) lemon juice

Method

1. Grease an 8″ loose bottom cake tin.
2. Melt the butter in a saucepan, add the crushed digestives, mix well. Press into cake tin. Chill.
3. Put lemon juice in a small ramekin. Sprinkle the gelatine over the lemon juice, allow to stand for 10 minutes.
4. Place ramekin in a sauce pan containing a small amount of simmering water (not boiling).
5. Lift up the ramikin, and gently shake to ensure all the gelatin granules are dissolved.
6. Place in the blender or food mixer the cream cheese, mascarpone cheese, crème fraîche and condensed milk. Mix together well. Fold in the cooled gelatine and marshmallows.
7. Pour over the biscuit base. Chill until set.

Cook's Note: *Serve with pouring cream.*

Ice Cream

Isabella's jams lend themselves really well to making ice cream. The following recipes were a great hit, when we was tested them, and are very easy to make. No fancy ice cream machine required, just a good old tupperware container with a lid.

Damson Jelly Ice Cream
1 Jar of Isabella's Damson Jelly and Gin Preserve
$\frac{1}{2}$ pt double cream
Juice of $\frac{1}{2}$ a lime
zest of an orange (grated)

Method

Combine the preserve with the lime juice, add the orange zest.
Whip the double cream till it is holding its shape.
Fold the two mixtures together.
Tip into a freezer container.
Use as required.

Lemonchello Ice Cream
1 Jar Lemonchello preserve
10 fl.oz ($\frac{1}{2}$ pt) Greek yogurt
50g (2oz) castor sugar
Juice of 1 orange

Method
Combine the lemonchello with the orange juice, stir in the castor sugar.
Fold in the Greek yogurt.
Turn into a freezer container. Use as required.

Cook's Note: *This goes well with a lemonchello roulade.*

Marmalade Ice Cream

1 jar Isabella's Seville Orange Marmalade
10 fl.oz ($^{1}/_{2}$ pt) double cream
Juice of 1 lemon

Method
Combine the lemon juice with the marmalade.
Whisk the double cream until just holding its shape.
Fold both mixtures together.
Pour into a freezer container.
Use as required.

Cook's Note: *This goes extremely well with the steamed marmalade sponge pudding. Page 65. A simple orange sauce is just the finishing touch required.*

Apricot and Tangerine Ice Cream

1 jar of Apricot and Tangerine Conserve
10 fl.oz ($^{1}/_{2}$ pt) half fat crème fraîche
1 tsp ground cinnamon
Juice of 1 lemon

Method
Combine the lemon juice with the conserve, add the cinnamon.
Lightly whip the double cream.
Fold together both mixtures.
Pour into a freezer container.
Use as required.

Cook's Note: *The apricot, tangerine and cinnamon are a surprisingly good combination. This one is my favourite.*

Wild Cherry and Bramble Ice Cream

1 jar Wild Cherry and Bramble Preserve
Juice and zest of 1 lime
5 fl.oz (¼ pt) double cream
5 fl.oz (¼ pt) single cream

Method
Combine the conserve with the juice and zest of the lime.
Stir in the single and double cream.
Turn into a freezer container.
Use as required.

Cook's Note: *The Wild Cherry preserve has an amazing texture and looks really nice when combined with other ingredients to make an ice cream. The lime helps to cut the sweetness of the preserve.*

Raspberry Ice Cream

1 jar Raspberry jam
5 fl.oz (¼ pt) Greek yogurt
5 fl.oz (¼ pt) double cream
Juice of 1 lemon
50g (2oz) castor sugar

Method
Combine the raspberry jam with the lemon juice.
Whip the double cream to hold its shape, fold in the greek yogurt.
Combine both mixtures, fold in the sugar.
Turn into a freezer container. Use as required.

Cook's Note: *The Strawberry jam can be used in this recipe with just as good results*

Marmalade Sponge Pudding
with
Marmalade Ice Cream

125g (4oz) butter
150g (5oz) castor sugar
200g (7oz) self raising flour
2-3 tablsp Seville Orange Marmalade

grated zest of 1 orange
2 eggs, beaten
juice of 2 oranges

Method

1. Prepare 6 x 150ml (5fl.oz.) moulds or one 900 ml (1½ pt) mould by greasing with butter.
2. For Steaming: use a saucepan large enough to hold the individual moulds or large mould.
3. In a baking bowl, cream the butter and castor sugar together, gradually adding the beaten egg, add the zest of orange, fold in the flour and stir in the orange juice.
4. Spread a teaspoonful of marmalade over the base of the individual moulds or 2-3 tablespoons over the larger one.
5. Spoon in the sponge mixture to fill ¾ of the way up the mould, snap on the plastic lids. Steam the individual puddings for about 35-40 minutes, the larger one for about 1¼ to 1½ hours.
6. Serve with the Seville Orange ice cream on page 63 of this book. An orange sauce is a nice addition to this recipe, it enhances the distinctly orange flavour.

Cook's Note: *This pudding is well worth the effort of having to keep topping up the steamer. Any marmalade can be used with good results.*

Apple Jalousie

Recipe from Clarissa Dickson Wright

"Everyone must make puff pastry at least once so that they have a choice whether to make it, or buy it.

The pudding takes its name from the effect of jalousies or blinds that is created by the cooked pastry. The word comes from the Norman, French to Look through. I like to think of those knights peering through their visors. It is an easy and delicious recipe and a great stand by of mine."

1 x 450g (1lb) packet or half the recipe for puff pastry
175g (6oz) Isabella's Three Fruit Marmalade
450g (1lb) cooking apples (peeled, cored and sliced)
Egg white to glaze
Castor sugar

Method

Roll out the pastry to a 30cm (12″) square. Cut in half and place one half on a greased baking sheet. Spread with the marmalade, leaving a 2.5cm (1″) margin all round, then cover the marmalade with the sliced apples.

Roll the remaining piece of pastry to a 33x8cm (13x8″) rectangle and fold in half length ways. Using a sharp knife cut into the fold at 1cm (¹/₂″) intervals, to within 2.5cm (1″) of the edge and ends. Brush the pastry margin with water, and position the lid over the apples, unfolding it to cover evenly. Fit the margins carefully together. Press all round with the flat of a knife, then scallop the edges.

Brush with egg white and dredge evenly with sugar. Bake in a pre-heated oven at 220°C, 425°F, Gas Mark 7 for 25-30 minutes, until well risen and golden brown. This can be made before dinner and put in to cook during the main course.

Chocolate Torte

250g (9oz) plain chocolate
25g (1oz) butter, melted
1 tablsp golden syrup
175g (6oz) amaretti biscuits

40g (1¹/₂oz) clear honey
12fl.oz. (360ml) double cream

Method

1. Grease a 20cm (8″) cake tin; line with baking parchment.
2. Place 50g (2oz) chocolate, sugar, butter and syrup in a bowl, set over a pan of gently simmering water; stir until melted.
3. Combine the melted chocolate mixture with the amaretti biscuits. Press firmly into the cake tin. Chill for 30 minutes.
4. Heat the honey, sugar and 3 tablespoonfuls of water in a small pan, slowly bring to the boil. Break up the remaining chocolate adding it to the mixture. Stir until smooth and melted.
5. Fold in the whipped cream.
6. Chill for 3-4 hours or until set.

To Serve: Remove the torte from the tin; peel off the parchment paper. Decorate with crushed amaretti biscuits and melted chocolate around the edge of the torte. Dust with cocoa powder.

Cook's Note: *For a special occasion the Lindt 70% cocoa solids,plain chocolate works well. However the chocolate of your choice will work just as well.*

THE BAKING SECTION

Marmalade Cake

125g (4oz) butter
125g (4oz) castor sugar
2 eggs
175g (6oz) self raising flour
1 tablsp Isabella's Seville Orange Marmalade
Milk for mixing

This recipe is Auntie Bella's fail me never recipe. It is easily doubled, and always a nice stand-by to have in the freezer.

Method

1. Pre-heat the oven to 180°C, 350°F, Gas Mark 4.
2. Line a 2lb loaf tin; with tinfoil.
3. Cream the butter and sugar together, gradually add the beaten eggs, and the marmalade.
4. Fold in the flour, if the mixture is too stiff add a little milk.
5. Bake for 45 minutes, or until well risen and pale golden on top.

Cooks Note: *This is delicious served as a dessert, warmed through with Marmalade Ice Cream; see page 65 for the recipe.*

Fruit Squares

Alastair's Mother's recipe

Fruit squares are commonly known by the name, "Fly Cemetery" in the North East of Scotland, fortunately the name bears no relation to the taste.

<u>Pastry</u>
225g (8oz) plain flour
125g (4oz) margarine, cut into cubes
cold water to mix

Method
Grease a 30x23cm (12x9″) tray bake tin. Pre-heat the oven to 180°C, 350°F, Gas Mark 4. In a large mixing bowl, sieve the flour. Add the margarine and rub the fat into the flour to resemble fine breadcrumbs. Add cold water by the tablespoon, mixing with a broad bladed knife, until the mixture starts coming together. Form into a ball. Knead lightly on a floured board. Cut in two and roll both pieces out to fit the tray bake tin. Line the base with one piece of the pastry and chill.

<u>Filling</u>

125g (4oz) currants	1 tsp ground ginger
125g (4oz) raisins	1 tsp ground cinnamon
50g (2oz) sugar	1 tsp cornflour
25g (1oz) mixed peel	³⁄₄ cup water
25g (1oz) stem ginger, chopped	

Method
Put all ingredients in a pan, and heat gently until the sugar has melted, cool.
Spread the filling over the pastry base, cover with the remaining pastry. Bake in the pre-heated oven until the pastry is light brown and crisp, 30-40 minutes. When cold, cut into squares and dust with castor sugar.

Banana Loaf

A very popular favourite with children and adults alike.

125g (4oz) butter
175g (6oz) soft brown sugar
2 eggs
2 tablsp hot milk
1 tsp bicarbonate of soda
1 tsp baking powder
225g (8oz) wholemeal flour
2 mashed bananas

Method

1. Pre-heat the oven to 150°C, 300°F, Gas Mark 3. Line a 20x10cm (8x4″) loaf tin with silicone baking paper or grease and flour the tin.
2. Cream the butter and sugar in a large mixing bowl, gradually adding the eggs and mashed banana.
3. Dissolve the bicarbonate of soda in hot milk and beat in.
4. Fold in the flour and baking powder.
5. Turn into the lined loaf tin and bake in the pre-heated oven for 45 minutes to 1 hour or until well risen and golden in colour.

Rock Buns

225g (8oz) self raising flour
¹/₂ tsp baking powder
65g (2¹/₂ oz) margarine
50g (2oz) sugar
1 tablsp Isabella's Apricot & Tangerine Preserve

25g (1oz) mixed peel
50g (2oz) mixed fruit
1 egg, beaten
1 tsp cinnamon
Milk to mix

Method

1. Pre-heat the oven to 180°C, 350°F, Gas Mark 4. Grease a baking tray 36x25cm (14x10″).
2. Sieve all dry ingredients into a large mixing bowl.
3. Rub the margarine into the dry ingredients
4. Blend to a stiff dough with the beaten egg, milk and Apricot and Tangerine Preserve.
5. Drop heaped tablespoonfuls on to the baking sheet. Bake in the pre-heated oven for 15-20 minutes.
6. Dust with cinnamon sugar while still hot. Transfer to wire cooling rack.

Cooks Note: *Isabella made these one morning when we were working on the cookbook. They are so good straight from the oven, with a nice cup of tea.*

Pancakes

Isabella is known as the "Queen" of preserves, however by the number of pancakes she makes she also reigns almighty in the pancake stakes.

250g (8oz) plain flour
50g (2oz) castor sugar
1½ tsp cream of tartar
¾ tsp bicarbonate of soda
1 egg
Milk to blend

Method

1. Sift all dry ingredients into a large bowl.
2. Beat the egg, add the milk.
3. Make a well in the dry ingredients, pour in the egg mixture.
4. Gradually incorporate the flour into the egg, to make a thick batter. Let stand a few minutes while the girdle heats.
5. When hot, grease the girdle with butter, drop dessert spoonfuls of batter on to the girdle. When bubbles rise to the surface of the pancake, flip it over, cook both sides until golden brown.
6. Pop the pancakes inside a tea towel, on a cooling rack.

This quantity makes approximately 20 pancakes.

Cooks Note: *Isabella makes her pancakes on the cool side of the Aga. Serve warm with Isabella's Raspberry Jam - Pure Heaven!!*

Shortbread Fingers

our grandaughter Flora's Favourite Recipe

225g (8oz) butter
225g (8oz) plain flour
125g (4oz) rice flour
125g (4oz) castor sugar

Method

1. Pre-heat the oven to 180°C, 350°F, Gas Mark 4.
2. Combine the flour, rice flour and castor sugar in a bowl.
3. Add the butter, and knead by hand, until the mixture becomes a soft dough, shape into a ball.
4. Roll out into a large square and cut into fingers. The fingers should be approximately 2cm ($^3/_4''$) thick and 7.5cm (3″) long.
5. Place on a baking sheet and prick with a fork to prevent rising.
6. Bake for 30 minutes or until evenly golden brown, dust with castor sugar.

Cooks note: *These can be seen in the colour section.*

Honey Oatie Biscuits

125g (4oz) butter
75g (3oz) soft brown sugar
Pinch of salt
125g (4oz) plain flour
125g (4oz) porridge oats
2 tsp honey
$\frac{1}{2}$ tsp bicarbonate of soda
$\frac{1}{2}$ tsp baking powder

Method

1. Pre-heat the oven to 180°C, 350°F, Gas Mark 4.
2. Melt together the butter, sugar and honey. Sift the flour, baking powder and soda into a bowl, add all other dry ingredients and mix well.
3. Pour the butter mixture over the dry ingredients, mix well, form into balls.
4. Flatten slightly with a fork on a baking sheet.
5. Bake for 10-15 minutes or until golden brown.

Cooks Note: *These are a great favourite when the children just come in the door from school, and healthy for them to eat.*

Chocolate Brownies

100g (3¹/₂oz) chopped pecans
100g (3¹/₂oz) butter, cut into rough pieces
100g (3¹/₂oz) plain chocolate, break into squares
225g (8oz) light brown sugar
2 eggs, beaten
55g (2oz) self raising flour

Method

1. Pre-heat the oven to 180°C, 350°F, Gas Mark 4. Line a 20cm (8″) square baking tin with non-stick parchment paper.
2. Bake the pecans for 6-8 minutes, until they are lightly browned and wonderful to smell. Cool.
3. Melt the butter and chocolate in a saucepan over a gentle heat. Remove from the heat and stir in the eggs, sugar and flour. Beat until smooth and stir in the pecan pieces.
4. Pour into the prepared baking tin and bake for about 30 minutes; the brownies should still be soft in the middle, but firm around the edges. Cool for a few minutes before trying to cut into squares. Remove from the tin using a spatula.

Cooks Note: *These may never get a spatula near them, they disappear so fast from the tin, and straight on to the waist-line, of course!!*

Raspberry Pecan Muffins

225g (9oz) self raising flour
1 tsp baking powder
$^1/_2$ tsp (2.5ml) salt
85-110g (3-4oz) castor sugar
Isabella's Raspberry Conserve 7x1 tsp

1 egg, beaten
240mls (8fl.oz.) milk
85g (3oz) melted butter
50g (2oz) pecan nuts, chopped
100g (3oz) white chocolate chips

Method

1. Pre-heat the oven to 190°C 375°F Gas 5-6.
2. Line a muffin tin with large muffin cases. The recipe yeilds 7 large muffins.
3. In a large baking bowl sieve together all the dry ingredients.
4. Combine the egg, milk and butter.
5. Pour over the dry ingredients, stir until just combined.
6. Stir in the pecan nuts and chocolate chips.
7. Half fill the muffin cases, add a teaspoon of preserve to each muffin case, top off with batter.
8. Bake for 20-25 minutes until well risen and brown. Cool on a wire baking rack.

Cooks note: *These are so easily made, a great American concept, which thankfully we have now adopted. Great lunch box food for the kids!!*

Peachy, White Chocolate Muffins

Isabella's preserves really lend themselves well to making muffins, these were a really pleasant surprise.

225g (9oz) self raising flour
1 tsp (15ml) baking powder
½ tsp (2.5ml) salt
85-110g (3-4oz) castor sugar
1 egg, beaten
240ml (8fl.oz) milk
85g (3oz) melted butter

100g (3oz) white chocolate chips
7 tsp Isabella's Peach Conserve with Brandy

Method

1. Pre-heat the oven to 190°C, 375°F, Gas Mark 5-6. Line a muffin tin with large muffin cases. Yield 7 large muffins.
2. In a large bowl, sieve together the dry ingredients.
3. Combine the egg, milk and butter.
4. Pour over the dry ingredients, stir until just combined. Stir in the chocolate chips.
5. Half fill the muffin cases, add a teaspoon of preserve to the muffin case, top off with batter.
6. Bake for 20-25 minutes till well risen and brown. Cool on a wire baking rack.

Cooks Note: *These are best eaten warm.*

Mini Cheese Scones

225g (8oz) plain flour
1 tsp cream of tartar
$\frac{1}{2}$ tsp bicarbonate of soda
1 egg yolk
50g (2oz) Mature Scottish Cheddar

60g (2$\frac{1}{2}$oz) margarine
2 tsp salt
Good pinch cayenne pepper
1 tsp mustard
2 tablsp Isabella's Mustard Relish

<u>Topping</u>
25g (1oz) grated cheddar

Method

1. Pre-heat the oven to 220°C, 450°F, Gas Mark 8.
2. Mix all the dry ingredients together in a large mixing bowl, rub in the margarine.
3. Add the cheese.
4. Blend together the egg yolk and milk.
5. Add to the mixing bowl, mix to a firm dough.
6. Roll out on a floured board, and cut out with a round fluted cutter, transfer to a baking tray.
7. Brush with milk and egg wash. Top with grated cheddar, mixed with Isabella's Mustard Relish.
8. Bake for 10-12 minutes. Serve hot.

Cooks Note: *These freeze well.*

Mini Mincemeat Pies

<u>Mincemeat</u>

To a 500gm (1lb) jar of mincemeat add

1 tsp mixed spice	125g (4oz) suet
500gm (1lb) mixed dried fruit	4 fl.oz. ($\frac{1}{2}$ cup) brandy

Mix well, leave for one month, stir occasionally.

<u>Shortcrust pastry</u>

300g (10oz) flour	cold water to mix
150g (5oz) butter	a pinch of salt

Method

Pre-heat the oven to 180°C, 375°F, Gas Mark 4.
Sieve the flour into a mixing bowl, cut the butter into cubes, add the the flour and rub in, until the mixture resembles fine bread crumbs. Add the cold water by the tablespoon.Using a broad bladed knife,bring the mixture together to form a ball. Wrap in cling film, chill for 30 minutes.
Roll the pastry out on a floured board. Using a round pastry cutter cut out in circles and line a tartlet case. Trim evenly into the case and trim edges. Prick the bases. Cover and rest in the fridge for 30 minutes. Fill with mincemeat. From the left over pastry, use a star cutter to cut out decorative stars, which can be placed on top of the mincemeat. Brush with milk and sprinkle with soft brown sugar. Bake in the pre-heated oven for 20-25 minutes or until the pastry is cooked.

Rich Christmas Cake

500g (1lb) sultanas
50g (2oz) crystallised pineapple
50g (2oz) raisins

225g (8oz) chopped glace cherries
50g (2oz) mixed peel

Place the above ingredients in a plastic box pour over 6fl.oz.(185ml) brandy, snap the lid on tight. Place in the fridge for 1-2 weeks stirring occasionally.

For the cake

180g (6oz butter)
180g (6oz) dark soft brown sugar
225g (8oz) plain flour
4 eggs
2fl.oz. brandy

½ tsp cinnamon
½ tsp nutmeg
125g (4oz) ground almonds
Grated rind of an orange

Method

1. Pre-heat the oven to 180°C, 375°F, Gas 4.
   Grease and line a 20cm (8inch) round cake tin, with silicone paper.
2. Cream the butter and sugar together, adding the eggs one at a time.
3. Then fold in the flour, ground almonds, grated rind and lastly the fruit. Stir well.
4. Tip into the lined cake tin, bake in the pre-heated oven for 2¼ hours, reduce the heat to 150°C, 300°F, Gas 3 and bake for a further hour. Remove from the oven and prick the surface with a skewer pour on 2fl.oz brandy. Leave to cool.
5. Remove from tin when cool, wrap in greaseproof paper and store in a cool place for a month before using.

Cooks Note: *This makes one large cake or 2 small, always useful presents at Xmas.*

Stockists of Isabella's products

Please note the following stockists are just a few of the many stores, which stock Isabella's range.

The Store, Foveran, Nr Ellon, Aberdeenshire	01358-788083
Haddo Estate Shop, Haddo House, Methlick	01651-851815
Baxters of Fochabers	01343-820393
Costcutters, Ellon, Aberdeenshire	01358-720281
Blairman's Farm Shop, Stirling	01259-762266
Bothy Antiques, Rait, Perthshire	01828-686617
Brechin Castle Centre	01356-626813
Brocksbushes Limited, Corbridge	01434-633100
Brodie Country Fayre, Forres	01309-641111
Butterchurn, Kelty, Fife	01383-830169
Brykley Park Centre, Burton on Trent	01283-716467
Crieff Visitor Centre	01764-654014
Deans of Huntly	01466-792086
Erskine Hospital Garden Centre	0141-8120657
The Food Library, Abernyte	01828-686848
GMTS Gretna Green	01461-337662
Glendoick Garden Centre	01738-860260
Gordon McPhail, Elgin	01343-545110
Gourmets Lair, Inverness	01463-225151
House of Bruar, Blair Athol	01796483236
House of Menzies, Aberfeldy	01887-829666
Jenners Edinburgh	0131-2252442

Stockists Continued

Scottish Liquer Centre, Bankfoot	01738-787044
Kirkland Nurseries, Arran	01770-700683
Loch Fyne Oysters, Argyll	01499-600264
Lochter Fishery, Oldmeldrum	01651-806630
Meadowlands Gallery, Banff	01261-818535
Morgan McVeighs, Huntly	01464-841399
NTS Culzean House Farm Shop	0131-2439300
Neish,Peterhead	01779-472721
Peel Farm, Kirriemuir	01575-560205
Raemoir Garden Centre, Banchory	01330-825059
Sandy Holm Nursery, Clyde Valley	01555-860205
Scone Palace Gift Shop, Perth	01738-552300
Scottish Antique's and Art Centre, Doune	01786-841203
Silverspoon Tearoom, Peebles	01721-720162
James Stewart, Lesmahagow	01555-893246
Summer Isle Foods, Auchiltibuie	01854-622353
Terrior, Aberdeen	01224-636555
The Kitchen Garden,Oban	01631-566332
Ceol na mara,Ullapool	01444-417651
The Wishing Well, Balfon	01360-551038
Mitchell's Dairy, Inverurie	01467-621389
Celebrations, Turriff	01888-568111
Scotch Corner, Turriff	01888-563079
Inverurie Garden Centre	01467-621402
Ardaran Farm Shop, Helensburgh	01389-849188
Kelly of Cults	01224-867596
Glamis Castle Gift Shop	01307-840393
Inverglen Gifts, Banchory	01330-820222
Pestle & Mortar, Blanefield	01360-771110
The Horn, Abernyte	01821-670216

Notes